This book starts with the guided basic alphabet to develop the required muscle memory and progressively advances to writing sentences. Is organized on 4 chapters:
1. Tracing lower case and uppercase letters of the alphabet
2. Tracing Words
3. Tracing Numbers
4. 101 Fun Facts

You can use a pencil or pen to trace the dotted numbers and letters.

Let's practice!

1. Alphabet

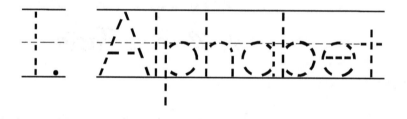

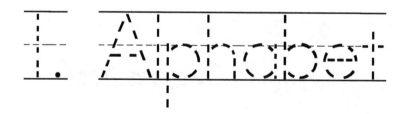

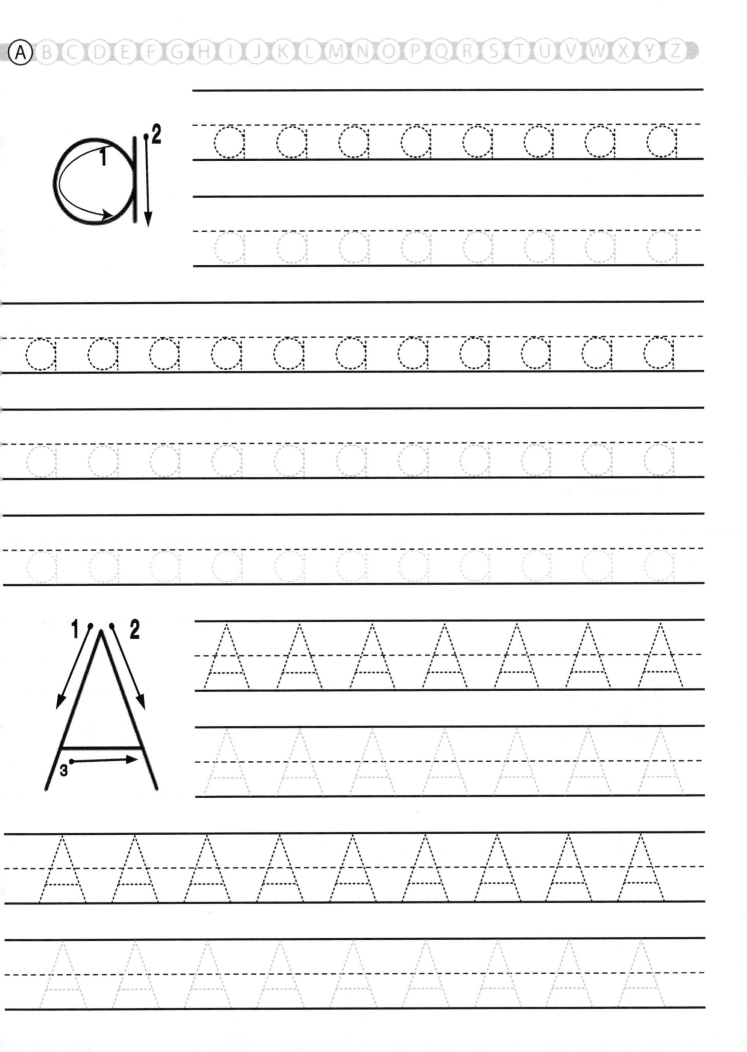

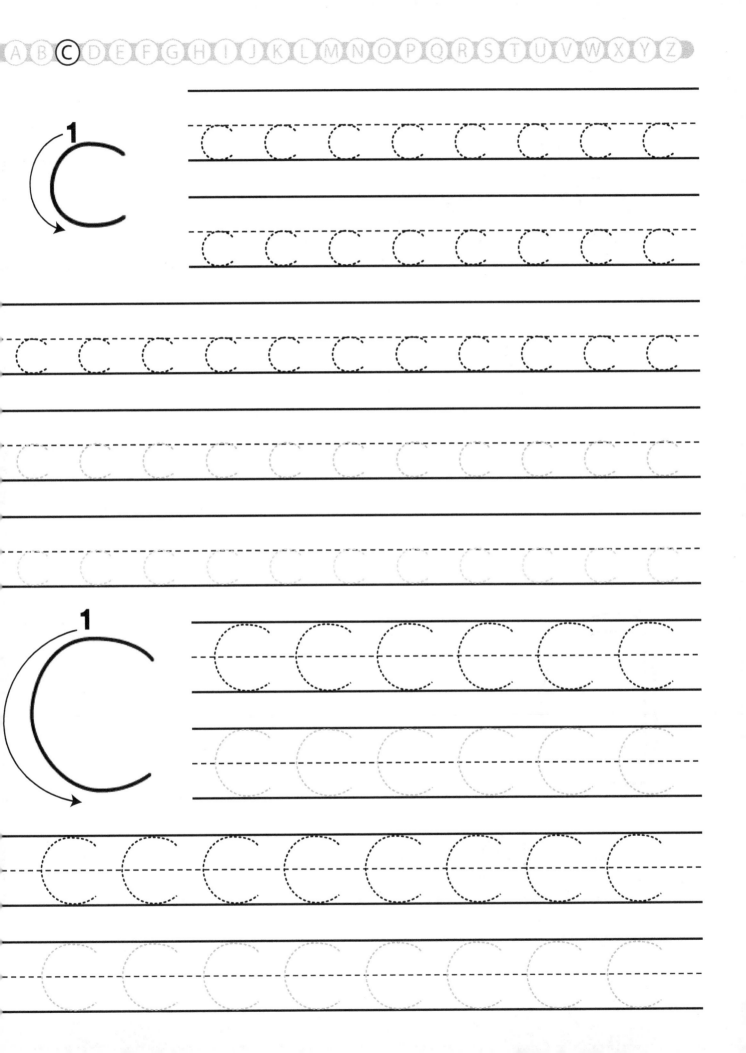

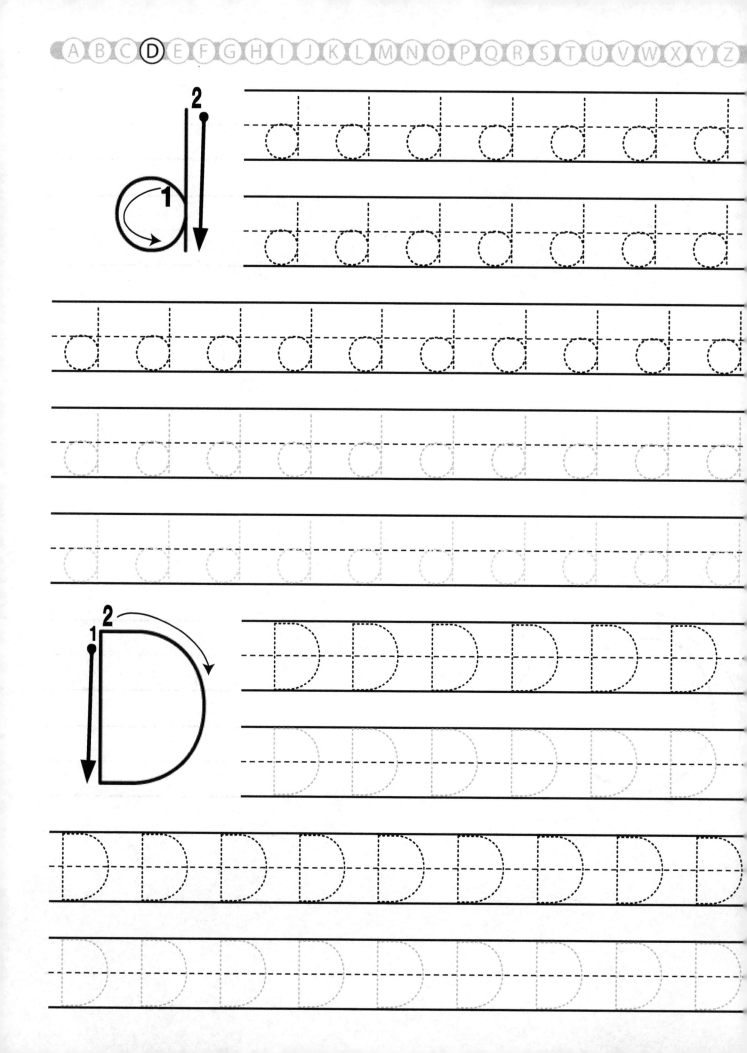

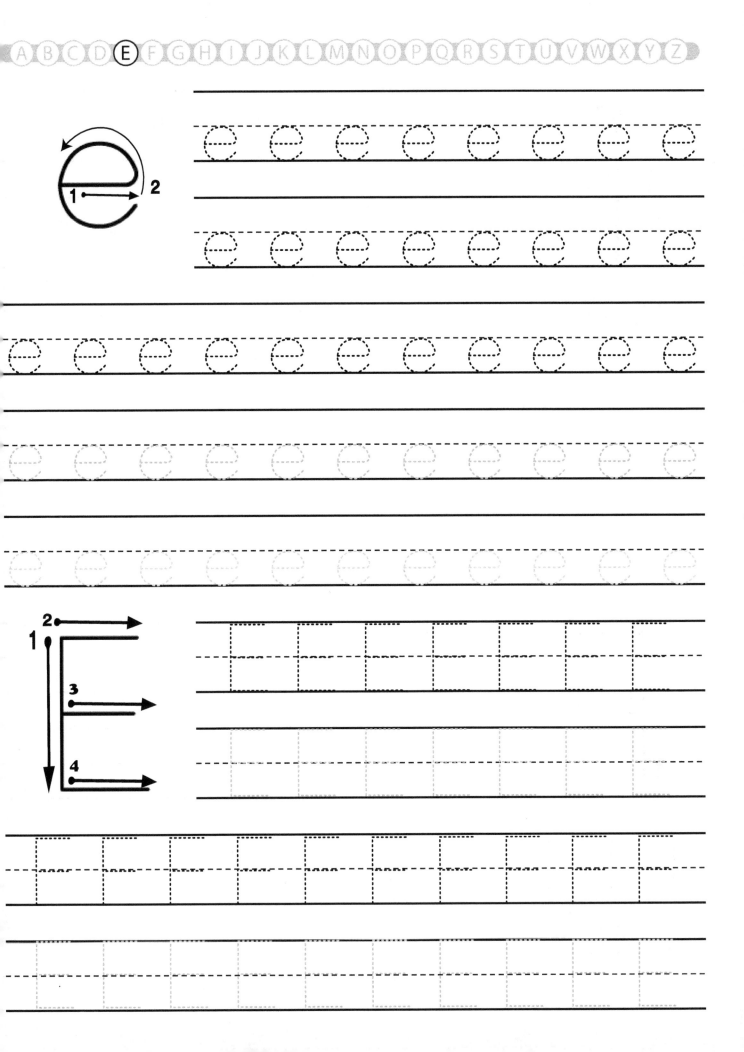

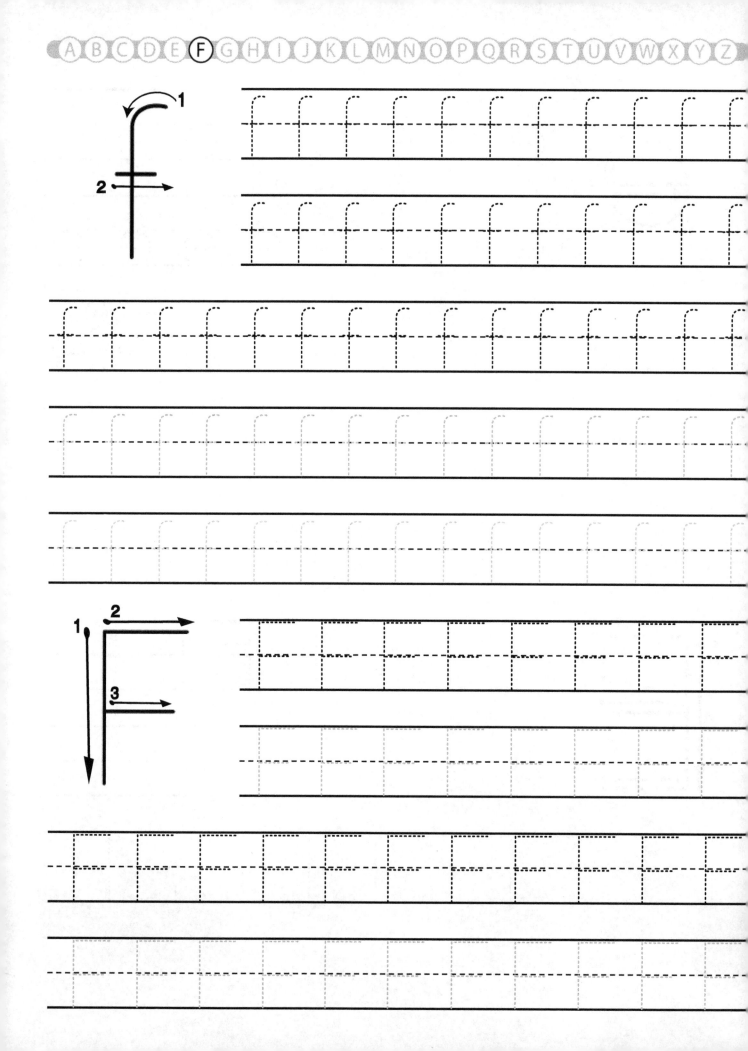

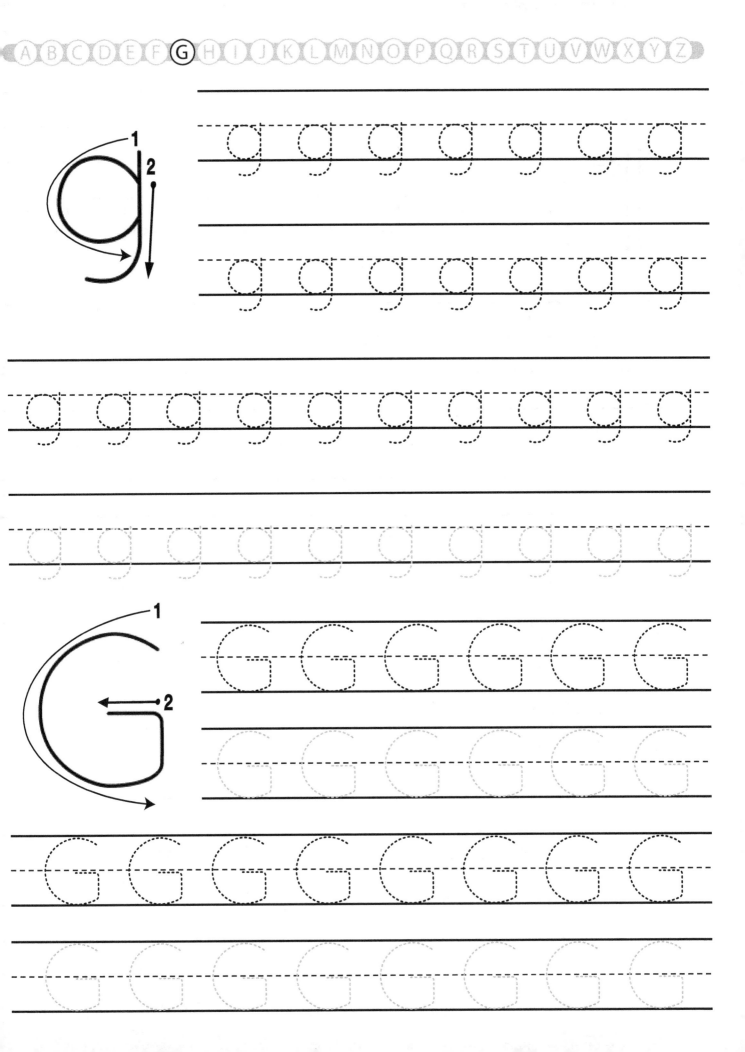

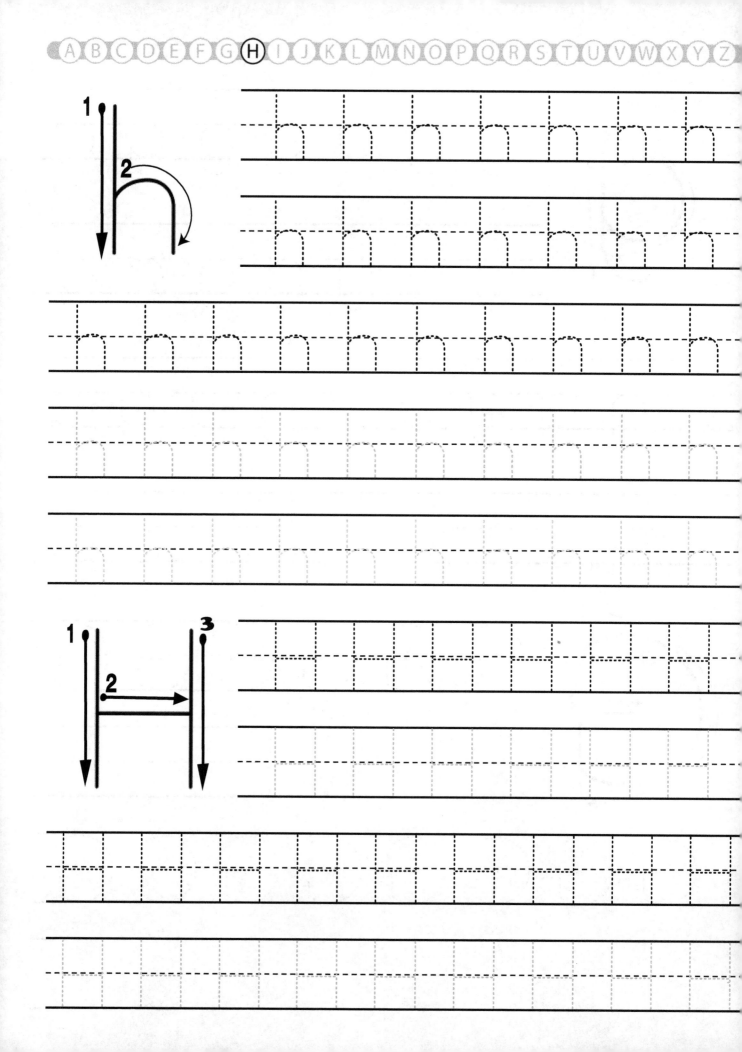

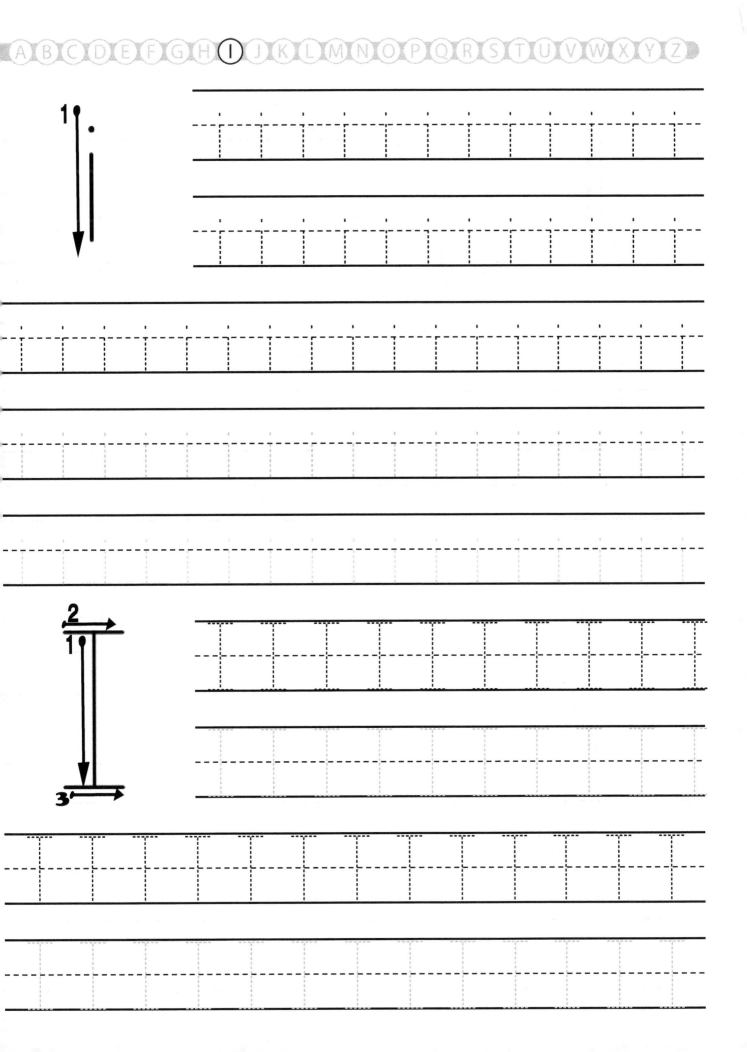

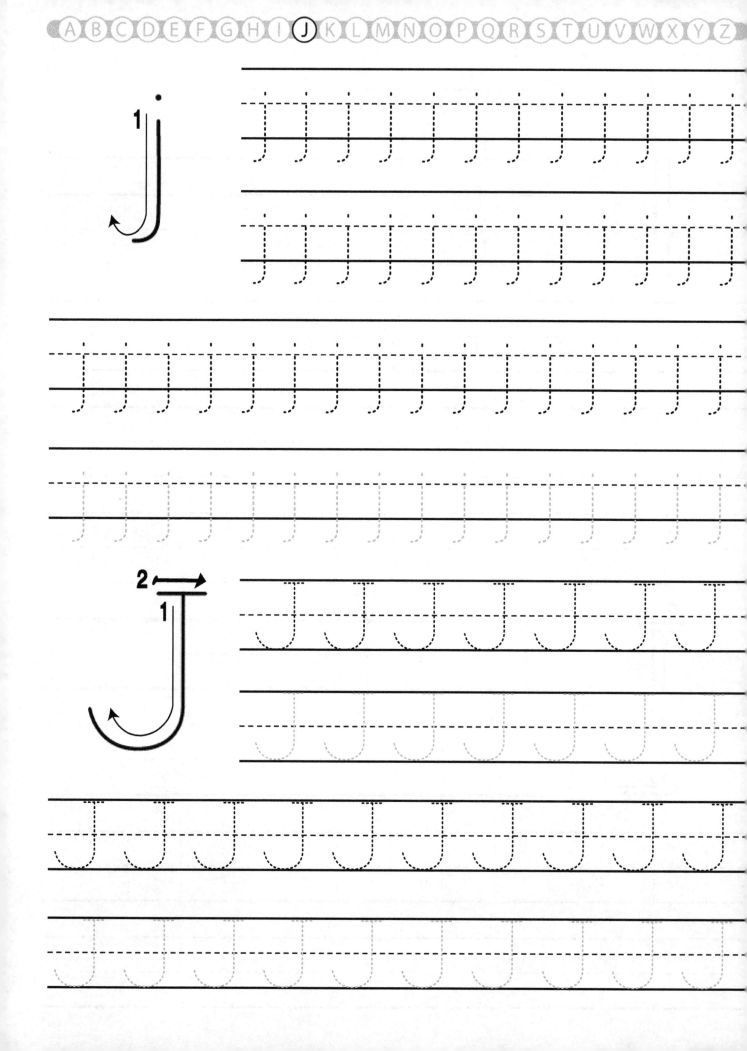

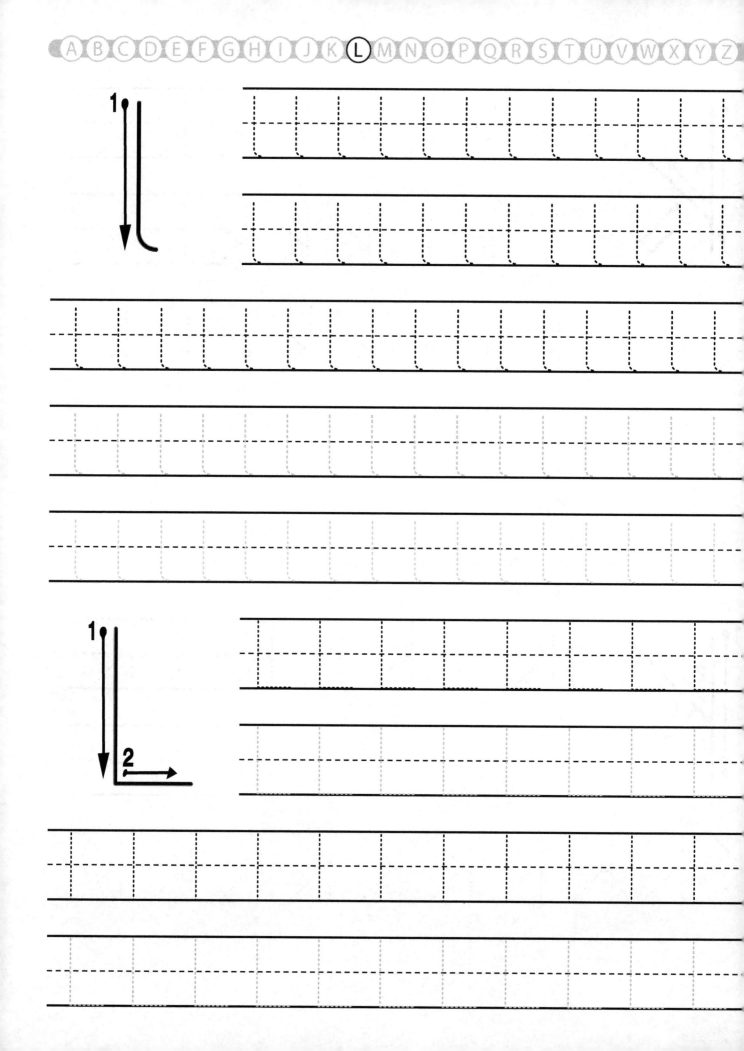

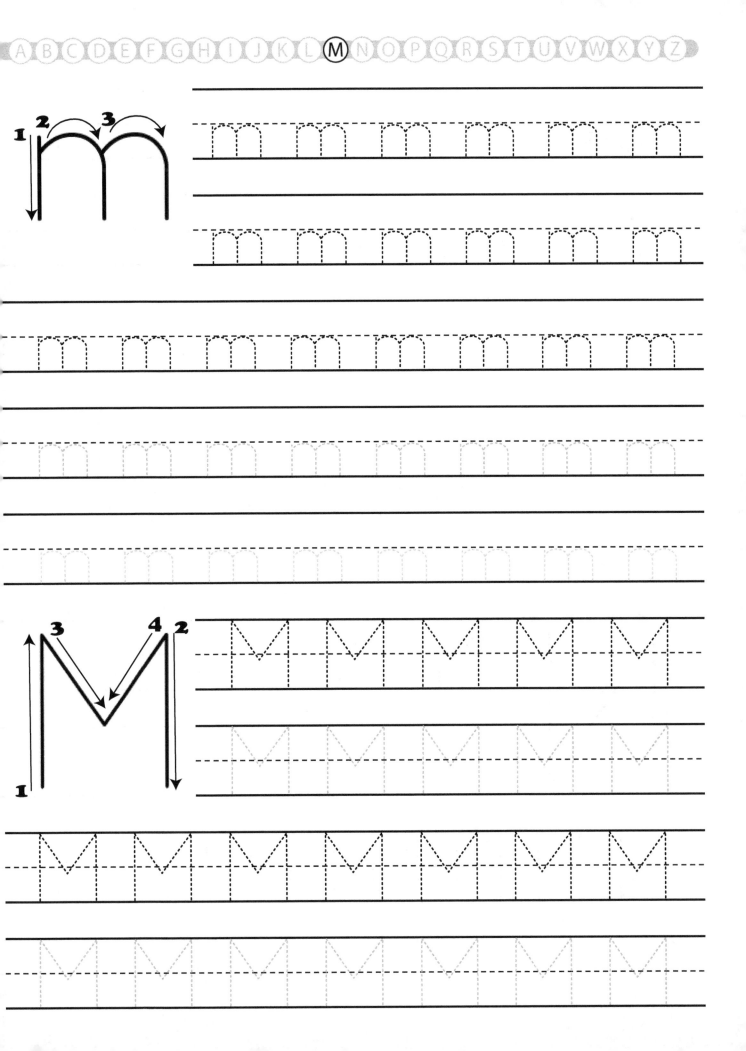

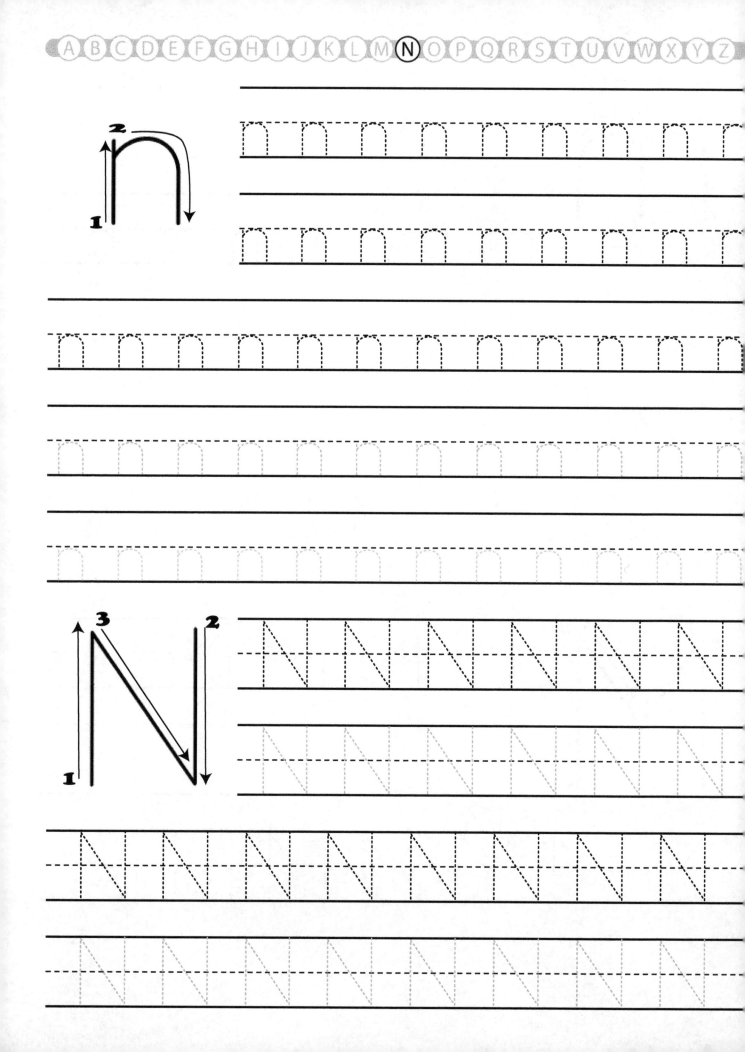

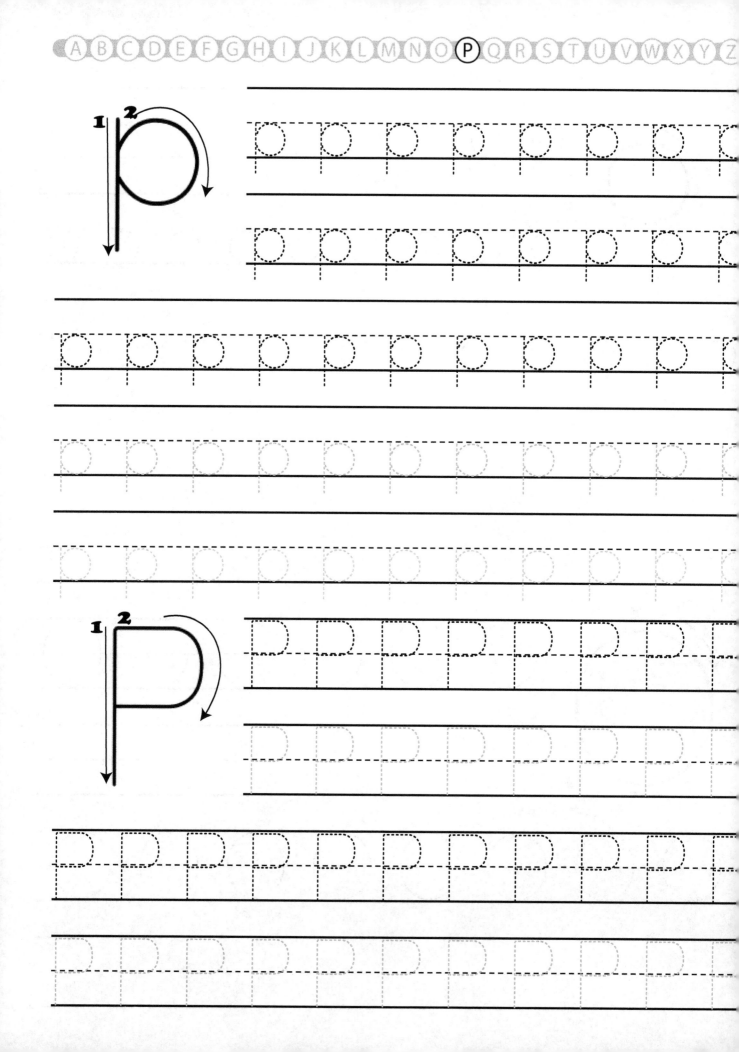

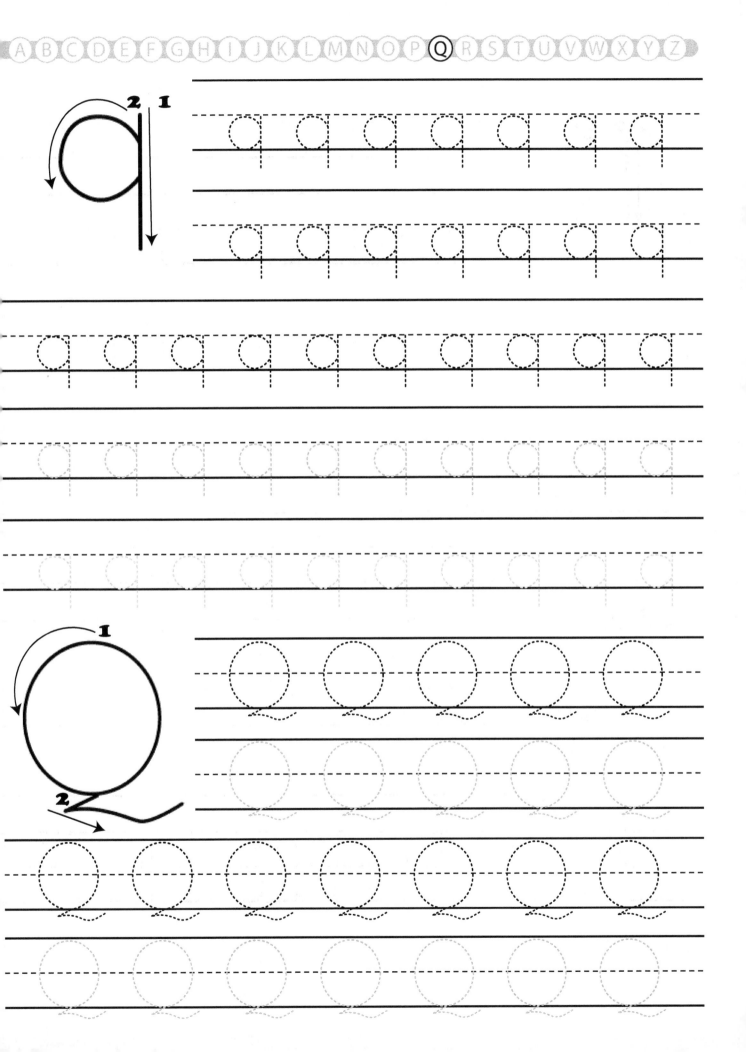

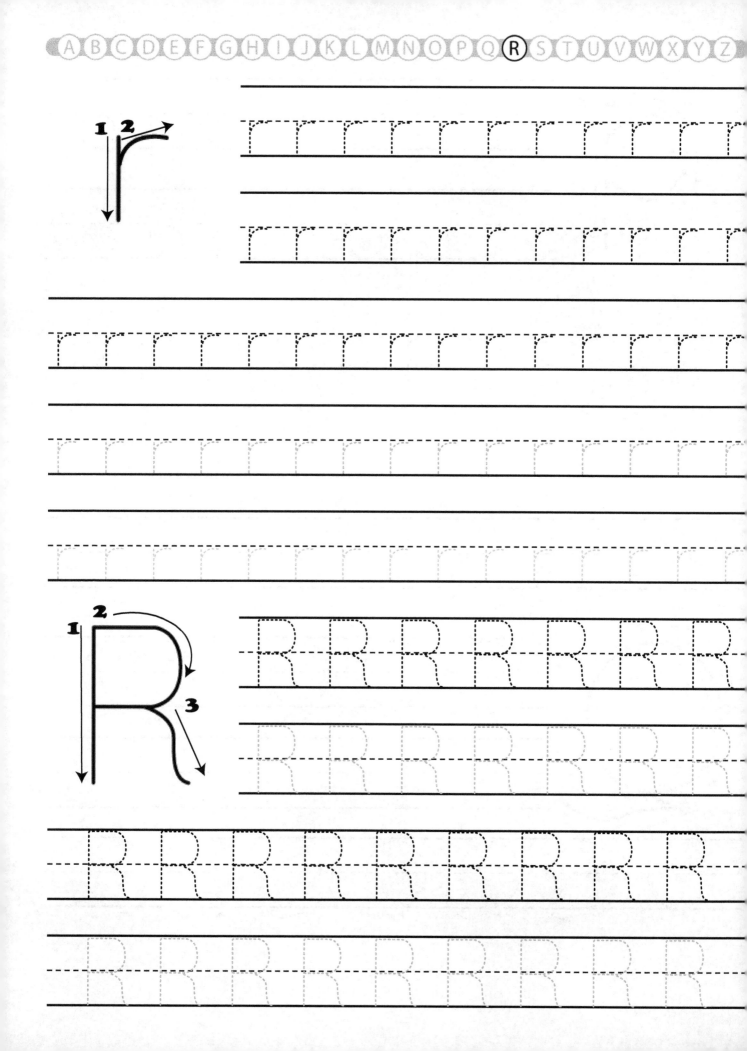

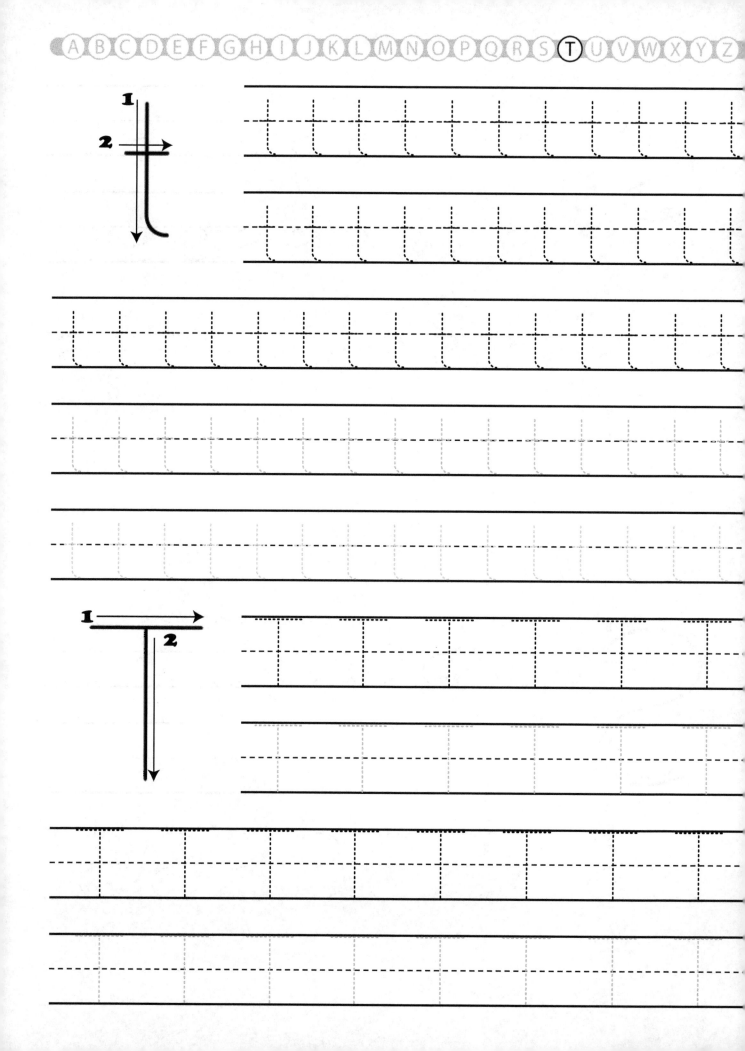

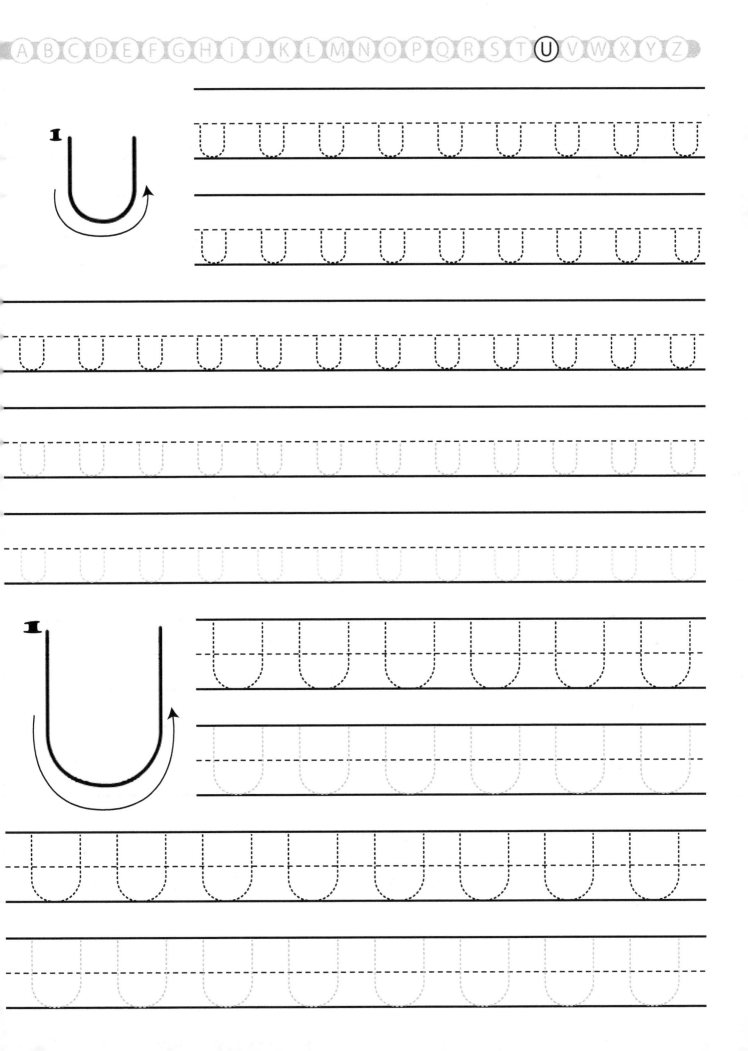

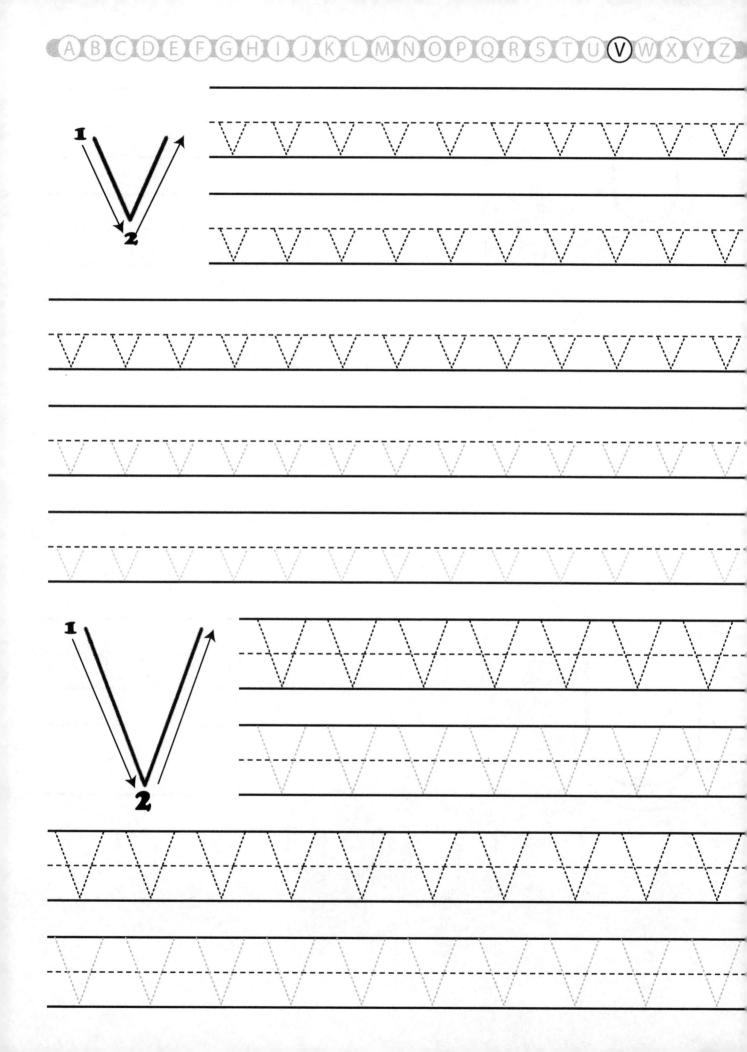

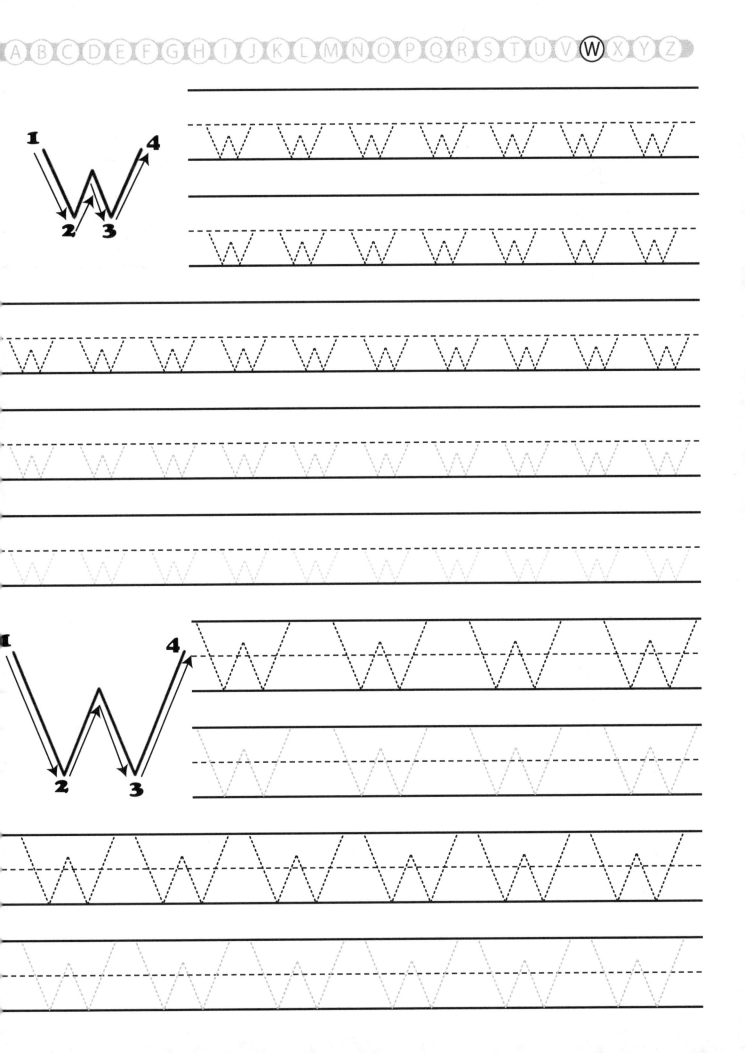

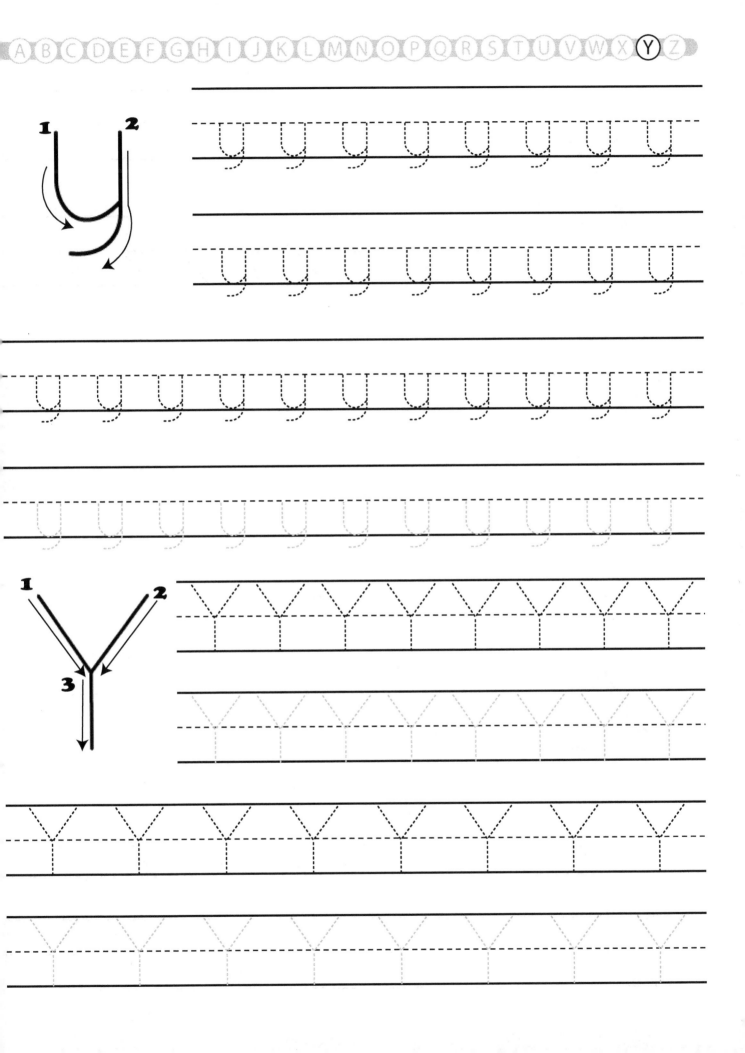

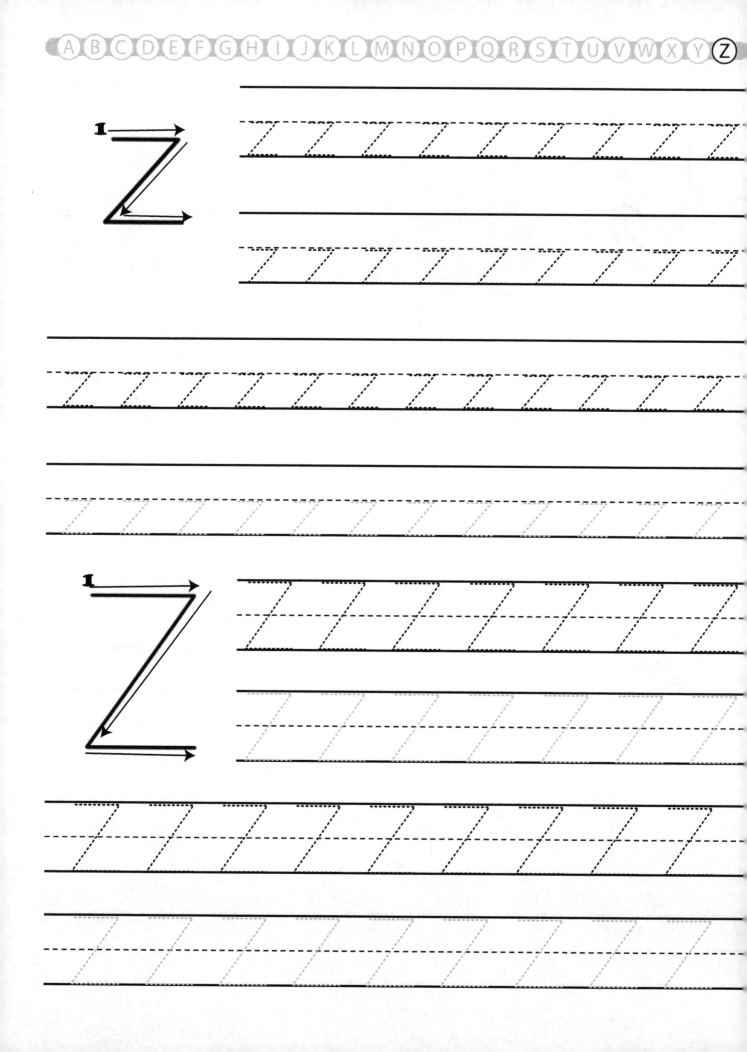

2. Words

2. Words

2. Words

eat eat eat eat eat eat eat eat

sleep sleep sleep sleep sleep sleep

love love love love love love love

dream dream dream dream dream

big big big big big big big big big

yes yes yes yes yes yes yes yes

yes yes yes yes yes yes yes yes

you you you you you you you you

work work work work work work

hard hard hard hard hard hard hard

don't don't don't don't don't don't

wait wait wait wait wait wait wait

it's it's it's it's it's it's it's it's it's it's

time time time time time time time

to to to to to to to to to to to to to

unleash unleash unleash unleash unleash

your your your your your your your

inner inner inner inner inner inner

dragon dragon dragon dragon dragon

you you you you you you you you

get get get get get get get get

what what what what what what

you you you you you you you you

focus focus focus focus focus focus

on on on on on on on on on on

3. Numbers

3. Numbers

3. Numbers

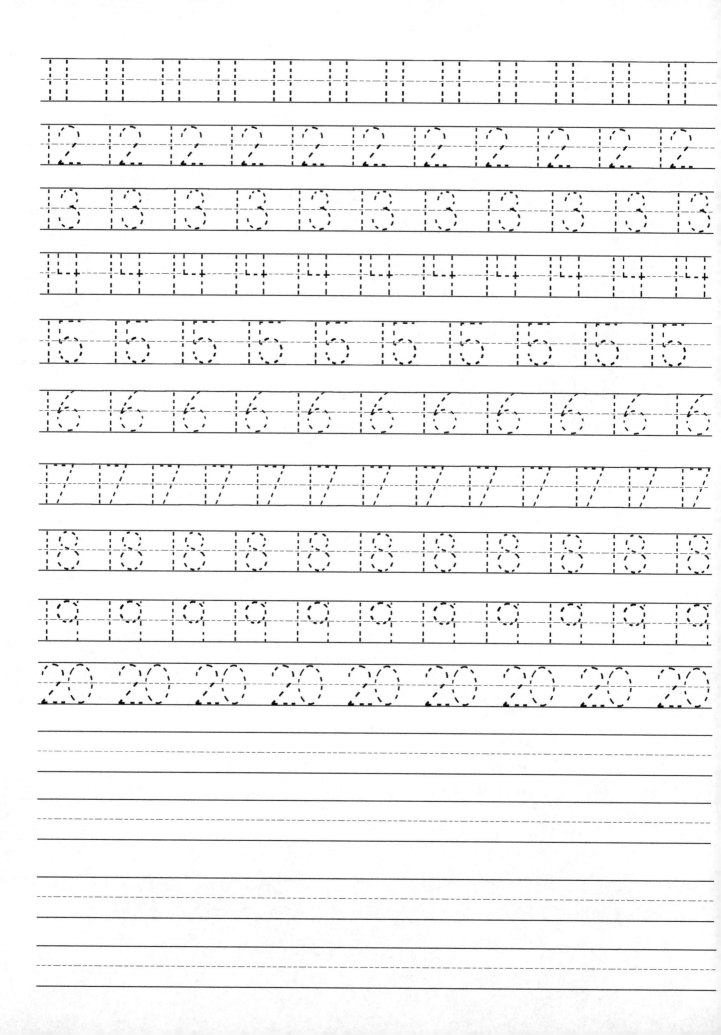

4. 101 Fun Facts

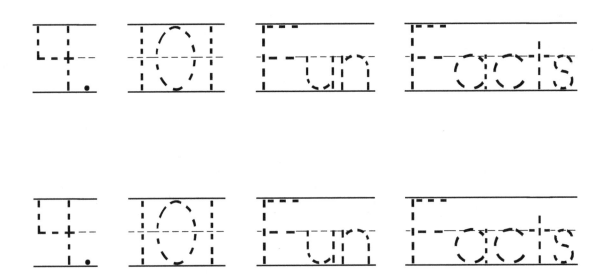

The Earl of Sandwich, John Montagu, who lived in the 1700s, reportedly invented the sandwich so he wouldn't have to leave his gambling table to eat.

_____

The oldest person ever to have lived (whose age could be authenticated), a French woman named Jeanne Louise Calment, was 122 years old when she died in 1997.

_____

The Four Corners is the only spot in the US where you can stand in four states at once: Utah, Colorado, Arizona and New Mexico.

The original name for the search engine Google was Backrub. It was renamed Google after the googol, which is the number one followed by 100 zeros.

The tallest living man is 37-year-old Sultan Kosen, from Turkey, who is 8 feet, 2.8 inches, who set the record in 2009. His growth is also due to a pituitary issue.

_____
_____
_____
_____
_____
_____
_____
_____
_____

The tallest man ever recorded was American giant Robert Wadlow (1918-1940), who stood 8 feet 11 inches. Wadlow's size was the result of abnormally enlarged pituitary gland

_____
_____
_____
_____
_____
_____
_____
_____
_____
_____

Three presidents, all Founding Fathers John Adams, Thomas Jefferson, and James Monroe died on July 4. Presidents Adams and Jefferson also died the same year, 1826. President Monroe died in 1831. Coincidence? You decide.

The Barbie doll's full name is Barbara Millicent Roberts, from Willows, Wisconsin. Her birthday is March 9, 1959, when she was first displayed at the New York Toy Fair.

There actually aren't "57 varieties" of Heinz ketchup, and never were. Company founder H.J. Heinz thought his product should have a number, and he liked 57. Hint: Hit the glass bottle on the "57," not the bottom, to get the ketchup to flow.

One of President John Tyler's grandsons is still alive today and he was born in 1790. How is this possible? President Tyler, the 10th US president, was 63 when his son Lyon Tyler was born in 1853. Lyon's son was born when he was 75. President Tyler's living grandson, Harrison Tyler is 92. Lyon's other son Lyon Jr. passed away in 2020 at the age of 95. The Tyler family still maintains the President's home, Sherwood Forest Plantation in Virginia.

Sliced bread was first manufactured by machine and sold in the 1920s by the Chillicothe Baking Company in Missouri. It was the greatest thing since...unsliced bread?

The first college football game was played on November 6, 1869, between Rutgers and Princeton (then known as the College of New Jersey) in New Brunswick, New Jersey. Rutgers won.

Experiments in universities have actually been carried out to figure out how many licks it takes to get to the center of a Tootsie Pop, both with machine and human lickers (because this is important scientific knowledge). The results ranged from 252 to 411.

Canada is south of Detroit (just look at a map).

Bats are the only mammal that can actually fly.

The oldest-known living land animal is a tortoise named Jonathan, who is 187 years old. He was born in 1832 and has lived on the island of St. Helena in the Atlantic Ocean since 1832.

The heart of the blue whale, the largest animal on earth, is five feet long and weighs 400 pounds. The whale in total weighs 40,000 pounds.

Wombats are the only animal whose poop is cube-shaped. This is due to how its intestines form the feces. The animals then stack the cubes to mark their territory.

The most common wild bird in the world isn't the sparrow or blue jay—it's the red-billed quelea, which live in Africa and have an estimated population of 1.5 billion.

For comparison, an elephant's heart weighs around 30 pounds. And a human heart? A mere 10 ounces.

Elephants can't jump.

Octopuses have three hearts.

Cows don't actually have four stomachs, they have one stomach with four compartments.

The platypus doesn't have a stomach at all. Their esophagus goes straight to their intestines.

This is one animal myth that's true. Eating part of a pufferfish can kill you because, in a defense mechanism to ward off predators, it contains a deadly chemical called tetrodotoxin. There's enough in one pufferfish to kill 30 people and there's no antidote. Still, pufferfish, called fugu, is a highly-prized delicacy in Japan, but can only be prepared by well trained chefs.

Polar bears have black skin. And actually, their fur isn't white—it's see-through, so it appears white as it reflects light.

Tigers' skin is actually striped, just like their fur. Also, no two fur patterns are alike.

Flamingoes are only pink because of chemicals called carotenoids in the algae and fish (which also eat the algae) they eat, their feathers are grayish white when they're born.

Mosquitoes are the deadliest animal in the world. They kill more people than any other creature, due to the diseases they carry.

What do Miss Piggy and Yoda have in common? They were both voiced by the same person, puppeteer Frank Oz.

Psycho was the first movie to show a toilet flushing.

One of the most famous movie lines in history was never said. We often quote, "Play it again, Sam," from Casablanca, but the real line is, "Play it, Sam. Play 'As Time Goes By.'"

The green code in The Matrix was actually created from symbols in the code designer's wife's sushi cookbook.

The wedding of Princess Diana and Prince Charles was watched by 760 million people worldwide in 1981; sadly, 2.5 billion watched her funeral in 1997.

With 3.572 billion viewers, half the world's population watched the 2018 FIFA World Cup of soccer (or football, as many international fans call it), which is held every four years. That number is on par with the 2016 Summer Olympics, but only a quarter of the world watched the less-popular Winter Olympics in 2018.

There are no muscles in your fingers. Their function is controlled by muscles in your palms and arms.

The hardest working muscle in your body is your heart. It pumps more than 2,000 gallons of blood a day and beats more than 2.5 billion times in a 70-year life span.

It's impossible to hum while holding your nose (just try it).

Skin is the body's largest organ.

The earth's circumference is 24,900 miles.

All of an adult human's blood vessels, if laid out
end to end, would be about 100,000 miles, so
they could encircle the earth four times.

According to recent research, the human nose
can distinguish at least a trillion different odors.

The longest fingernails ever were over 28 feet
in total. American Lee Redmond started growing
them in 1979 and set the record in 2008. Sadly,
she lost her nails in a car crash in 2009.

The origin of the word "sinister" reflects a historical bias against left-handed people. It comes from the Latin word for "left," which was also seen to be unlucky or evil.

There is not one letter "q" in any US state name, the only letter in the alphabet to be missing. "J" and "Z" are only represented once each, in New Jersey and Arizona.

The word "strengths" is the longest word in the English language with only one vowel.

Cartoonist Mort Walker, creator of Beetle Bailey, came up with names for the things we often see in comics and cartoons: "briffit" is the dust cloud a character makes when he runs away quickly, "plewds" are the beads of sweat when a character is under duress, and "grawlix" are symbols such as "#@*%" that stand in for curse words.

The original title of Jane Austen's Pride and Prejudice was First Impressions.

A mash-up of two words to make a new word (such as breakfast and lunch into brunch, or motel from motor and hotel) is called a portmanteau. In case youre wondering, the word "portmanteau" itself is not a portmanteau, its a compound word that refers to a duel-sided suitcase.

Hawaiian pizza was created in Ontario, Canada, by Greek immigrant Sam Panopoulos in 1962.

The dog ate John Steinbeck's homework literally. The author's pup chewed up an early version of Of Mice and Men. "I was pretty mad, but the poor fellow may have been acting critically," he wrote.

Among lost works, this story might be even worse. Ernest Hemingway's first wife, Hadley, left a suitcase full of the author's writing on a train. When she went back to get it, it was gone. "I had never seen anyone hurt by a thing other than death or unbearable suffering except Hadley when she told me about the things being gone," Hemingway wrote in A Moveable Feast.

Mary Shelley wrote Frankenstein when she 18, during a ghost story competition while staying in Switzerland with writers Percy Shelley (her lover) and Lord Byron.

German chocolate cake doesn't come from Germany. It was named for a person, Sam German, who created a type of baking chocolate for Baker's in 1852.

The different colors of Froot Loops cereal all taste the same—they're not individual flavors.

Almost all commercially grown artichokes, 99.9 percent, come from California. One town in particular, Castroville, is nicknamed "the Artichoke Capital of the World."

What's inside a Kit Kat? Broken Kit Kats that are damaged during production they get ground up and go between the wafers inside, along with cocoa and sugar. That's a way to not let anything go to waste!

Pound cake got its name because the original recipe required a pound each of butter, flour, sugar and eggs. That's a lot of cake but it was meant to last for a long time.

The difference between jam and jelly is that jam is made with mashed up fruit while jelly is made with fruit juice.

Preserves are like jam but made with more whole fruit. Marmalade is preserves made from citrus fruit.

Flamin' Hot Cheetos were developed by a janitor at Frito-Lay, Richard Montanez, who got the idea after putting chili powder on some reject Cheetos and then pitched it to the CEO. He's now a successful executive and motivational speaker, and a movie is in the works about his life.

Coca-Cola actually sells soup in a can. Bistrone is a nourishing meal on the go, available in two flavors in Japan.

The biggest pizza ever created was 13,580 square feet, made in Rome, Italy, in 2012. The pizza was gluten-free and named "Ottavia" after a roman emperor.

The tallest building in the world is the Burg Khalifa in Dubai, standing at over 2,700 feet.

The tallest building in the US is One World Trade Center in New York, which comes in at number six on the worldwide list. It stands at exactly 1,776 feet as a nod to the date of the Declaration of Independence.

The Empire State Building in New York was the tallest building in the world from 1931 until 1971, and was the first building of over 100 floors.

Contrary to popular belief, it's really, really hard to see the Great Wall of China from space, particularly with the naked eye.

Days on Venus are longer than years. Due to its slow axis rotation, it takes 243 Earth days to spin once, but it only takes 225 Earth days to go around the sun.

The first footprints on the moon will remain
there for a million years.

Humans could never "land" on Jupiter, Saturn,
Uranus or Neptune because they are made
of gas and have no solid surface.

But you could ice skate on one of Jupiter's
moons, Europa, which is covered in ice. An
Axel jump would take you 22 feet in the air.

Queen Victoria's husband, Prince Albert, wasn't the first to introduce Christmas trees to Britain from his native Germany Queen Charlotte did that in the late 1700s. But, Victoria and Albert are credited with popularizing the custom in the mid-1800s.

Buckingham Palace in London, England, has 775 rooms, including 78 bathrooms.

The White House in Washington, DC, has 132 rooms, including 35 bathrooms.

It takes 570 gallons to paint the exterior of the White House.

The teddy bear is named after President Theodore Roosevelt. After he refused to shoot a captured black bear on a hunt, a stuffed-animal maker decided to create a bear and name it after the president.

Lincoln Logs were created by John Lloyd Wright, son of famous architect Frank Lloyd Wright, in the 1920s. They were named after Abraham Lincoln, who grew up in a log cabin.

Play-Doh started out as a wallpaper cleaner before the head of the struggling company realized the non-toxic material made a good modeling clay for children and rebranded it.

In the 1940s, a retired schoolteacher came up with Candyland to entertain children who were hospitalized from polio. Because its color system required no reading, young kids could easily play.

People started wearing pajamas, originally
spelled "pyjamas," instead of nightgowns so
they'd be prepared to run outside in public
during World War I air raids in England.

At Medieval Times dinner attractions, you eat
with your hands because people didn't use utensils in the middle ages.

Freelancers originally referred to
self-employed, sword-wielding mercenaries:
literally "free lancers."

People started wearing pajamas, originally spelled "pyjamas," instead of nightgowns so they'd be prepared to run outside in public during World War I air raids in England.

At Medieval Times dinner attractions, you eat with your hands because people didn't use utensils in the middle ages.

Freelancers originally referred to self-employed, sword-wielding mercenaries, literally "free lancers."

Although no longer connected to the beer company, Guinness World Records was founded by the managing director of Guinness Brewery in the 1950s.

Michelin stars are highly coveted by elite and upscale restaurants the world over but they're actually given out by the Michelin tire company, the same one whose mascot is the marshmallow-like Michelin Man. If you want to get fancy, pronounce it in the original French, "mich-LEH."

We shake hands to show we're unarmed.

More people visit France than any other country (Spain is second, the US third).

You can still stay at the world's oldest hotel, Nisiyama Onsen Keiunkan in Japan, which was founded in 705 AD.

The coldest temperature ever recorded occurred in Antarctica, -144 Fahrenheit, as reported by researchers in a scientific journal in 2018.

The longest place name in the word, at 85
letters, is "Taumatawhakatangihangakoauauota-
mateaturipukakapikimaungahoro-
nukupokaiwhenuakitanatahu," New Zealand.
Locals just call it Taumata Hill.

The hottest temperature ever recorded occurred in Furnace Creek, Death Valley, California, at 134 degrees Fahrenheit on July 10,
1913.

Japan records the most earthquakes of any country in the world, but the most earthquakes actually occurs in Indonesia.

Sweden has 267,570 islands, the most of any country in the world.

Each year 16 million thunderstorms happen around the world, and at any given moment, there are about 2,000 thunderstorms in progress.

Australia contains a number of pink lakes, but the most stunning is the Pepto Bismol-colored Lake Hiller. The color may be the result of certain algae.

At over 29,000 feet tall, Mt. Everest is the highest point on Earth, but it doesn't compare to the deepest point on Earth, the Mariana Trench, which is over 36,000 feet deep—nearly seven miles in the Pacific Ocean.

This isn't exactly a "fun" fact, but there are over 200 dead bodies of climbers on Mt. Everest because it's so difficult to bring them down.

Only two people have ever swum the entire length of the 2,350-mile Mississippi River. Slovenian long-distance swimmer Martin Strel in 2002 and American former Navy SEAL Chris Ring in 2015. Strel swam for 68 days in a row. Ring took one day off a week, taking 181 days.

Visitors are not allowed to scatter loved ones' ashes at Disney World or Disneyland. This is apparently a problem particularly around the Haunted Mansion attraction.

There's a world record for the holder of the most world records: Ashrita Furman, who's set more than 600 records and currently holds more than 200. His records have ranged from fastest mile on a pogo stick, longest time to hula hoop underwater and greatest distance traveled on a bicycle balancing a milk bottle on thehead.

The man who designed the Pringles can, Fred Bauer, is buried in one—or at least some of his ashes are.

Thank you,

Penciol is a small family company, started initially by parents who felt inspired by their kid's enthusiasm for discovery and learning. We strongly believe the number one factor for a child's educational success is an involved parent.

Later on, as we are passionate about creating cute and practical books, we started designing also for adults. Our mission is simple: provide our customers with authentic, creative, and unique products that are high quality, yet affordable. We design each book individually and always try to have some added value for meeting customer needs.

Your opinion about this book is very important for us, but also for future clients, so we invite you to write your feedback in the review section.

Feel free to reach out at penciolpress@gmail.com

Your reviews are very important to us and future clients!

CPSIA information can be obtained
at www.ICGtesting.com
Printed in the USA
LVHW050312140521
687425LV00014B/1231